Club Grolier

A Short Hand-List of English Plays, Masques, and Pageants

From the time of Queen Elizabeth to the restoration

Club Grolier

A Short Hand-List of English Plays, Masques, and Pageants
From the time of Queen Elizabeth to the restoration

ISBN/EAN: 9783337323523

Printed in Europe, USA, Canada, Australia, Japan

Cover: Foto ©ninafisch / pixelio.de

More available books at **www.hansebooks.com**

A Short Hand-List of English Plays, Masques, and Pageants, from the time of Queen Elizabeth to the Restoration. Printed, but not published, for the use of the Publication Committee of The Grolier Club. New-York, December, 1893.

A Short Hand=List of English Plays, Masques, and Pageants from the time of Queen Elizabeth to the Restoration

ALEXANDER, Sir William, Earl of Stirling.

1	The tragedy of Darius.	Edinburgh,	1603
2	do	London,	1604
3	The Alexandraean, a tragedie.	London,	1605

4 The Monarchicke tragedies.
              viz.: Croesus. ⎫
                   Darius. ⎭   1604

5 The Monarchicke tragedies.
              viz.: Croesus. ⎫
                   Darius. ⎪
                   The Alexandraean. ⎬   1607
                   Julius Caesar. ⎭

6	The Monarchicke tragedies. Third edition.	1616
7	Recreations with the muses.	1637

3

ARMIN, Robert.

  8 Two maids of More Clacke.   1609

BARCLAY, Sir William.

  9 The lost lady.   1638

BARNES, Barnaby.

  10 The devil's charter.   1607

BARON, Robert.

  11 Mirza.   n. d.

BARRY, Lodowick.

  12 Ram Alley.   1611

  13   do   1636

  14   do   1639

BEAUMONT and FLETCHER.

  15 Works.   1647

  16   do   1679

  17 Philaster.   1620

  18   do   1628

  19   do   1634

  20   do   1639

  21 The Maid's tragedy.   1619

22	The Maid's tragedy.	1622
23	do	1630
24	do	1638
25	do	1641
26	do	1650
27	do	1661
28	A king or no king.	1619
29	do	1625
30	do	1631
31	do	1639
32	do	1655
33	do	1661
34	The scournful lady.	1616
35	do	1625
36	do	1630
37	do	1635
38	do	1639
39	do	1651
40	The elder brother.	1637
41	do	1637
42	do	1651
43	do	1661
44	do	1678
45	The faithful shepherdess.	1629

46	The faithful shepherdess.	1634
47	do	1656
48	do	1665
49	do	n. d.
50	Wit without money.	1639
51	do	1661
52	Monsieur Thomas.	1639
53	The bloody brother.	1639
54	Rollo, Duke of Normandy.	1640
55	Rule a wife and have a wife.	1640
56	Knight of the burning pestle.	1613
57	do	1635
58	The night walker.	1640
59	do	1661
60	Cupid's revenge.	1615
61	do	1630
62	do	1635
63	Two noble kinsmen. (By FLETCHER and SHAKESPEARE.)	1634
64	Thierry and Theodoret.	1621
65	do	1648
66	do	1649
67	The woman hater.	1607
68	do	1648
69	do	1649

70 The beggar's bush.   1661

71   do   1717

72 Masque of Grayes Inn and the Inner Temple.   n. d.

BELCHIER, DABRIDGECOURT.

73 Hans Beer Pot.   1618

BIRKHEAD, HENRY.

74 Colas Fury.   1646

BRANDON, SAMUEL.

75 The virtuous Octavia.   1598

BRATHWAITE, RICHARD.

76 Mercurius Britannicus.   1641

BREWER, ANTONY.

77 The country girl.   1647

78 The love-sick king.   1655

BROME, ALEXANDER.

79 The cunning lovers.   1654

BROME, RICHARD.

80 The northern lass.   1632

81   do   1635

82 The northern lass.   1663

83   do   1684

84 The sparagus garden.   1640

85 The antipodes.   1640

86 A jovial crew.   1652

87   do   1684

88   do   1686

89 The Queen's exchange.   1657

90   do   1661

91 Five new plays:
         viz.: Mad couple well matcht.
               Novella.
               Court beggar.   1653
               City wit.
               Damoiselle.

92 Five new plays:
         viz.: The English moor.
               Love-sick court.
               Covent garden weeded.   1659
               The new academy.
               Queen and Concubine.

BULTEEL, JOHN.

93 London's triumph.   1656

BURNELL, HENRY.

94 Landgartha.   Dublin, 1641

CAMPION, THOMAS.

95 Description of a maske in honour of Lord Hayes. 1607

96 Relation of the royal entertainment given by Lord

    Knowles. 1613

97 Description of a maske. (Squire's masque.) 1614

CAREW, LADY ELIZABETH.

98 Marian, the fair queen of Jewry. 1613

CAREW, THOMAS.

99 Coelum Britannicum. 1634

CARLELL, LODOWICK.

100 The deserving favorite. 1629

101   do 1639

102 Arviragus and Philicia. 1639

103 The passionate lover. 1655

104 Heraclius. 1664

105 Two new plays:
    viz.: The fool would be a favorite. ⎱
    Osmond the great Turk.   ⎰ 1657

CARPENTER, RICHARD.

106 The pragmatical jesuit new leavened. n. d.

CARTWRIGHT, George.

CARTWRIGHT, William.

CHAMBERLAIN, Robert.

CHAMBERLAIN, William.

CHAPMAN, George.

123 Bussy d'Ambois.   1616

124   do   1641

125   do   1646

126   do   1657

127 Tragedy of Charles, Duke of Byron.   1608

128   do   1625

129 May day.   1611

130 The widow's tears.   1612

131 Revenge of Bussy d'Ambois.   1613

132 Masque of the Middle Temple.   n. d.

133 Caesar and Pompey.   1631

134   do   1631

135   do   1653

    Chabot.   See Shirley.

    The ball.   See Shirley.

CHETTLE, HENRY.

136 Hoffman.   1631

    The blind beggar of Bethnall green.   See Day.

    The death of Robert Earl of Huntington.   See
      Munday.

    Patient Grissel.   See Dekker.

COCKAIN, SIR ASTON.

137 The obstinate lady.   1657

DAVENANT, Sir William.

154	Albovine.	1629
155	The cruel brother.	1630
156	The temple of love. (With Inigo Jones.)	1634
157	The triumphs of the Prince d'Amour.	1635
158	The platonic lovers.	1636
159	The wits.	1636
160	Britannia triumphans. (With Inigo Jones.)	1637
161	The just Italian.	1630
162	Salmacida Spolia.	1639
163	The unfortunate lovers.	1643
164	Love and honour.	1649
165	The siege of Rhodes.	1656
166	do	1659
167	First day's entertainment at Rutland House.	1657
168	The man's the master.	1669

169	Two excellent plays:
	             viz.: The wits.
	                    The platonick lovers.
		1665

170	Works.	1673

DAVENPORT, Robert.

171	A new trick to cheat the devil.	1639
172	King John and Queen Matilda.	1655

173	King John and Queen Matilda.	1662
174	The city nightcap.	1661

DAVIES, RICHARD.

175	Chester's triumph in honor of her prince.	1610

DAY, JOHN.

176	The isle of gulls.	1606
177	do	1633
178	The travels of three English brothers.	1607
179	Humour out of breath.	1608
180	Law tricks, or who would have thought it.	1608
181	The parliament of bees.	1641
182	The blind beggar of Bethnall Green.	1659

DEKKER, THOMAS.

183	The shoemaker's holiday.	1600
184	do	1610
185	do	1618
186	do	1631
187	do	1657
188	Old Fortunatus.	1600
189	Satiromastix.	1602
190	Patient Grissel. (With Haughton and Chettle.)	1603
191	Entertainment given to King James.	London, 1604

192	Entertainment given to King James.	Edinburgh, 1604
193	The honest whore. (With Middleton.)	1604
194	do	1605
195	do	1615
196	do	1616
197	do	1635
198	The whore of Babylon.	1607
199	Troia nova triumphans.	1612
200	Britannia's honor.	1628
201	London's Tempe.	1629
202	The second part of the honest whore.	1630
203	Match me in London.	1631
204	If it be not good the devil is in it.	1612
205	The wonder of a kingdom.	1636
206	The sun's darling. (With Ford.)	1656
207	do	1657

Northward Hoe.	See Webster.
Westward Hoe.	See Webster.
Sir Thomas Wyat.	See Webster.
The roaring girl.	See Middleton.
The witch of Edmonton.	See Ford.

DENHAM, Sir John.

208	The Sophy.	1642

D'OUVILLY, George Gerbier.

209 The false favorite disgraced. 1657

DRUE, Thomas.

210 The Duchess of Suffolk. 1631

DUGDALE, Gilbert.

211 The time triumphant. 1604

FIELD, Nathaniel.

212 Amends for ladies. 1618

213   do 1639

    The fatal dowry. See Massinger.

FISHER, Jasper.

214 The true Trojans. 1633

FLETCHER, Phineas.

215 Sicelides. 1631

FORD, John.

216 The lover's melancholy. 1629

217 'Tis pity she's a whore. 1633

218 Love's sacrifice. 1633

219 The broken heart. 1633

220 Perkin Warbeck. 1634

221 The fancies chaste and noble.   1638

222 The ladies trial.   1639

223 The witch of Edmonton.   (With Dekker.)   1638

     The sun's darling.   See Dekker.

FORDE, Thomas.

224 Love's labyrinth.   1660

FOUNTAIN, John.

225 The rewards of virtue.   1661

FREEMAN, Sir Ralph.

226 Imperiale.   1639

227   do   1655

FULWELL, Ulpian.

228 Like will to like.   1568

229   do   1587

GARTER, Thomas.

230 Susanna.   1578

GASCOIGNE, George.

231 The glass of government.   1575

GAYTON, Edm.

232 Charity triumphant.   1655

GLAPTHORNE, Henry.

233 Argalus and Parthenia.   1639
234 Albertus Wallenstein.   1639
235   do   1640
236 Wit in a constable.   1640
237 The Hollander.   1640
238 The ladies privilege.   1640

GOFFE, Thomas.

239 The raging Turk.   1631
240 The courageous Turk.   1632
241 Orestes.   1633
242 Three excellent tragedies.   1656
243 The careless shepherdess.   1656

GOMERSAL, Robert.

244 Ludovick Sforza.   1628
245   do   1633

GOUGH, John.

246 The strange discovery.   1640

GREENE, ROBERT.

247	Orlando Furioso.	1594
248	do	1599
249	Friar Bacon and Friar Bungay.	1594
250	do	1599
251	do	1630
252	do	1655
253	do	1666
254	James the fourth.	1598
255	Alphonsus of Arragon.	1599
256	The Pinner of Wakefield.	1599

A looking-glass for London and England. See Lodge.

GREVILLE, FULKE, LORD BROOKE.

257	Mustapha.	1609

HABINGTON, WILLIAM.

258	The Queen of Arragon.	1640

HARDING, SAMUEL.

259	Sicily and Naples.	1640

HAUGHTON, WILLIAM.

260	Englishmen for my money, or, a woman will have her will.	1616

261 Englishmen for my money, or, a woman will
    have her will.   1626

262   do   1631
    Patient Grissel.   See Dekker.

HAUSTED, PETER.

263 The rival friends.   1632

HAWKINS, WILLIAM.

264 Apollo shroving.   1627

HEAD, RICHARD.

265 Hic et ubique ; or, the humours of Dublin.   1663

HEMING, WILLIAM.

266 The fatal contract.   1653

267 The Jew's tragedy.   1662

HEYWOOD, JOHN.

268 The play of love.   An interlude.   John Waley. n. d.

269 The pardoner and the friar.   1533

270 The play of the weather.   1533

271   do   n. d.

272 The four PP.   Middleton. n. d.

| 273 | The four PP. | Copland. | n. d. |
| 274 | do | Allde. | 1569 |

HEYWOOD, Thomas.

275	Edward IV.	1600
276	do	1605
277	do	1613
278	do	1619
279	do	1626
280	If you know not me, you know nobody. Part I.	1605
281	do	1606
282	do	1608
283	do	1613
284	do	1632
285	do	1639
286	If you know not me, you know nobody. Part II.	1606
287	do	1623
288	do	1633
289	do	1639
290	The fair maid of the exchange.	1607
291	do	1625
292	do	1634
293	do	1637
294	A woman killed with kindness.	1607

295	A woman killed with kindness.	1607
296	do	1617
297	The rape of Lucrece.	1608
298	do	1609
299	do	n. d.
300	do	1630
301	do	1638
302	The golden age.	1611
303	The silver age.	1613
304	The brazen age.	1613
305	The four prentices of London.	1615
306	do	1632
307	The fair maid of the west. Two parts.	1631
308	London's jus Honorarium.	1631
309	The iron age. Two parts.	1632
310	Londini artium et scientiarum origo.	1632
311	Londini emporia.	1633
312	The English travellers.	1633
313	A maidenhead well lost.	1634
314	The late Lancashire witches.	1634
315	Londini sinus salutis.	1635
316	Love's mistress.	1636
317	do	1640
318	do	1640

319 A challenge for beauty. 1636

320 The royal king and the loyal subject. 1637

321 Londini speculum. 1637

322 Pleasant dialogues and dramas. 1637

323 Porta pietatis. 1638

324 The wise woman of Hogsdon. 1638

325 Londini status pacatus. 1639

326 Fortune by land and sea. 1655

HOLIDAY, BARTEN.

327 Technogamia. 1618

328   do 1630

HOWELL, JAMES.

329 Nuptials of Peleus and Thetis. 1654

INGLELAND, THOMAS.

330 The disobedient child. (c. 1565)

JONES, JOHN.

331 Adrasta. 1635

JONSON, BEN.

332 Works. 1616

333 Works, 2 vols. 1640

334	Works.		1692
335	Every man out of his humour.	Ling.	1600
336	do	Home.	1600
337	Every man in his humour.		1601
338	Cynthia's revels.		1601
339	Poetaster.		1602
340	A particular entertainment of the Queen and Prince.		1603
341	Entertainment to King James.		1604
342	Sejanus.		1605
343	Hymenoei.		1606
344	Volpone.		1607
345	The character of two royal masques.		n. d.
346	The case is altered.		1609
347	The masque of Queens.		1609
348	Epicoene.		1609
349	do		1612
350	do		1620
351	Catiline.		1611
352	do		1635
353	The alchemist.		1612
354	The masque of augurs.		1621
355	Love's triumph through Callipolis.		1630
356	Chloridia: rites to Chloris and her nymphs.		1630

357 The new inn.   1631

     Eastward Hoe.   See Chapman.

     The widow.   See Middleton.

JORDAN, Thomas.

358 The walks of Islington and Hogsdon.   1657

359 Fancy's festivals.   1657

360 Money is an ass.   1668

361 A new droll; or, the counterscuffle.   1663

362 The goldsmith's jubilee.   1674

KILLIGREW, Henry.

363 The conspiracy.   1638

                                               1653

KILLIGREW, Thomas.

364 The prisoners.   1641

365 Claracilla.   1641

366 Comedies and tragedies.   1664

KILLIGREW, Sir William.

367 Pandora.   1664

368 The imperial tragedy.   1669

369 Three plays: viz.: Selindra.
                         Pandora.   1665
                         Ormasdes.

370 Three plays. Second edition. 1674

371 Four new plays: viz.: The siege of Urbin.
Selindra.
Love and friendship. } Oxford. 1666
Pandora.

KINASTON, Sir Francis.

372 Corona Minervae. 1635

KIRKE, John.

373 The seven champions of Christendom. 1638

KIRKMAN, Francis.

374 The wits, or sport upon sport. 1672–3

KNEVETT, Ralph.

375 Rhodon and Iris. 1631

KYD, Thomas.

376 Cornelia. 1594

377   do 1595

378 The Spanish tragedy. 1594

379   do n. d.

380   do 1599

381   do 1602

382   do 1602

383	The Spanish tragedy.		1610
384	do		1611
385	do		1623
386	do		1633
387	Jeronimo.		1605

LODGE, Thomas.

388	The wounds of civil war.		1594
389	A looking-glass for London and England. (With Greene.)		1594
390	do		1598
391	do		1602
392	do		1617

LOWER, Sir William.

393	The phoenix in her flames.		1639
394	Polyeuctes.		1655
395	Horatius.		1656
396	The enchanted lovers.	Hague.	1658
397	do	London.	1659
398	The noble ingratitude.	Hague.	1659
399	The amorous phantasm.	Hague.	1660
400	Three new plays.	London.	1661

LUPTON, Thomas.

   401 All for money.   1578

LYLY, John.

   402 Alexander and Campaspe.   1584

   403   do   1584

   404   do   1591

   405 Sapho and Phaon.   1584

   406   do   1591

   407 Endimion.   1591

   408 Galatea.   1592

   409 Midas.   1592

   410 Mother Bombie.   1594

   411   do   1598

   412 A woman in the moon.   1597

   413 Love's metamorphosis.   1601

   414 Six court comedies.   1632

MANUCHE, Cosmo.

   415 The loyal lovers.   1652

   416 The just general.   1652

   417 The Bastard.   1652

MARKHAM, Gervase.

   418 The dumb knight.   1608

419	The dumb knight.	1633
420	Herod and Antipater. (With W. Sampson.)	1622

MARLOWE, CHRISTOPHER.

421	Tamburlaine. Part I.	1590
422	do	1590
423	do	1592
424	do	1593
425	do	1597
426	do	1605
427	Tamburlaine. Part II.	1590
428	do	1592
429	do	1597
430	do	1606
431	Edward II.	1594
432	do	1598
433	do	1612
434	do	1622
435	Doctor Faustus.	1604
436	do	1609
437	do	1611
438	do	1616
439	do	1620
440	do	1624

441	Doctor Faustus.	1631
442	do	1663
443	Dido, Queen of Carthage. (With Nash.)	1594
444	Rich Jew of Malta.	1633
445	Massacre at Paris.	n. d.

MARMION, SHACKERLEY.

446	Holland's leaguer.	1632
447	do	1633
448	A fine companion.	1633
449	The antiquary.	1641

MARSTON, JOHN.

450	Antonio and Mellida.	1602
451	Antonio's revenge.	1602
452	The malcontent. (With Webster.)	1604
453	do	1604
454	The Dutch courtezan.	1605
455	Parasitaster.	1606
456	do	1606
457	Sophonisba.	1605
458	do	1606
459	What you will.	1607
460	The insatiate countess.	1613

461 The insatiate countess.   1616

462   do   1631

463 Works.   1633

       Eastward Hoe.   See Chapman.

MASON, John.

464 The Turk.   1610

                                                         1632

MASSINGER, Philip.

465 The virgin martyr.   1622

466   do   1631

467   do   1654

468   do   1661

469 The Duke of Milan.   1623

470   do   1638

471 The bondman.   1624

472   do   1638

473   do   1638

474 The Roman actor.   1629

475 The picture.   1630

476 The renegado.   1630

477 The emperor of the east.   1632

478 The maid of honor.   1632

479 The fatal dowry.   (With Field.)   1632

480 A new way to pay old debts.   1633

481 The great Duke of Florence.   1636

482 The unnatural combat.   1639

483 The city madam.   1658

484   do   1659

485 Three plays: viz.: A very woman. ⎫
                         The bashful lover. ⎬   1655
                         The guardian.   ⎭

     The old law.   See Middleton.

MAY, Thomas.

486 The heir.   1622 (?)

487   do   1633

488 Antigone.   1631

489 Julia Agrippina.   1639

490 Cleopatra.   1639

491 The old couple.   1658

492 Two tragedies: viz.: Cleopatra. ⎫
                          Agrippina. ⎭   1654

MAYNE, Jasper.

493 The city match.   1639

494   do   1658

495 The amorous war.   1648

496   do   1659

MEAD, ROBERT.

497 The combat of love and friendship.   1654

MERITON, THOMAS.

498 Love and war.   1658

MIDDLETON, THOMAS.

499 Blurt, Master Constable.   1602

500 The phoenix.   1607

501   do   1630

502 Michaelmas terme.   1607

503   do   1630

504 A trick to catch the old one.   1608

505   do   1608

506   do   1616

507 The familie of love.   1608

508 Your five gallants.   n. d.

509 A mad world, my masters.   1608

510   do   1640

511 The roaring girle.   (With Dekker.)   1611

512 The triumphs of truth.   1613

513   do   1613

514 Civitatis amor.   1616

515 Triumphs of honor and industry.   1617

516	A faire quarrel. (With Rowley.)		1617
517	do		1617
518	do		1622
519	Triumphs of love and antiquity.		1619
520	The Inner Temple masque.		1619
521	The world tost at tennis.		1620
522	The sun in Aries.		1621
523	Honourable entertainment composed for the service of this noble city.		1621
524	Triumphs of honor and virtue.		1622
525	Triumphs of integrity.		1623
526	Triumphs of health and prosperity.		1626
527	A chast mayd in Cheape-side.		1630
528	The widow. (With Jonson and Fletcher.)		1652
529	A game at chess.	Leyden.	n. d.
530	do	Leyden.	n. d.
531	do	Leyden.	n. d.
532	do	London.	n. d.
533	The changeling.		1653
534	do		1668
535	The Spanish gipsy.		1653
536	do		1661
537	The old law. (With Massinger and Rowley.)		1656
538	No wit, no help like a womans.		1657

539 The mayor of Quinborough. 1661

540 Anything for a quiet life. 1662

541 Two new plays:
        viz.: More dissemblers besides women. ⎫
            Women beware women. ⎬ 1657
                                    ⎭

    The honest whore.   See Dekker.

MILTON, JOHN.

542 Comus. 1637

MONTAGUE, WALTER.

543 The shepherd's paradise. 1659

MUNDAY, ANTONY.

544 The death of Robert Earl of Huntington.   (With
     Chettle.) 1601

545 Reunited Britannia. 1605

546 Camp-bell, or the Ironmongers' fair field. 1609

547 Chrysothriambos. 1611

548 Old drapery. 1614

549 Himatia-Poleos. 1614

550 Metropolis coronata. 1615

551 Chrysanaleia. 1616

552 Sideto-Thriambos. 1618

553 Triumphs of the golden fleece. 1623

NABBES, Thomas.

554	Microcosmus.	1637
555	Hannibal and Scipio.	1637
556	Tottenham Court.	1638
557	do	1639
558	Covent Garden.	1638
559	do	1639
560	The spring's glory.	1638
561	do	1639
562	The bride.	1640
563	The unfortunate mother.	1640

NAILE, Robert.

564	Entertainment to Queen Anne.	1613

NASH, Thomas.

565	Summer's last will and testament.	1600
	Dido. See Marlowe.	

NELSON, T.

566	Device of the fishmongers' pageant.	1590

NEVILE, Robert.

567	The poor scholar.	1622
568	do	1662

NEWCASTLE, Duchess of.

569 Plays. 1662–8

NEWCASTLE, Duke of.

570 The country captain. 1649

571 The variety. 1649

572 The humorous lovers. 1677

573 The triumphant widow. 1677

PALSGRAVE, John.

574 Acolastus. 1540

PEAPS, William.

575 Love in its extasy. 1649

PEELE, George.

576 The device of the pageant, &c. 1585

577 Polyhymnia. 1590

578 Descensus Astraeae. 1591

579 Edward I. 1593

580   do 1599

581 Battle of Alcazar. 1594

582 The old wives' tale. 1595

583 The love of King David and fair Bethsabe. 1599

PICKERING, JOHN.

584 Orestes: a new interlude of vice.   1567

PORTER, HENRY.

585 Two angry women of Abington.   1599
586   do   1599

PORTER, THOMAS.

587 The witty combat.   ·   1663
588 The carnival.   1664

PRESTON, THOMAS.

589 Cambyses.   n. d.
                                                                n. d.

QUARLES, FRANCIS.

590 The virgin widow.   1649
591   do   1656

RANDOLPH, THOMAS.

592 The jealous lovers.   1632
593   do   1634
594 Aristippus.   1630
595   do   1630
596   do   1631
597   do   1635

RAWLINS, Thomas.

  598 The rebellion.   1640

  599   do   1654

RICHARDS, Nathaniel.

  600 Messalina.   1640

RIDER, William.

  601 The twins.   1655

ROBERTS, Henry.

  602 Entertainment of the King of Denmark.   1606

  603 England's farewell to Christian the fourth. 1606

ROWLEY, Samuel.

  604 When you see me, you know me.   1605

  605   do   1613

  606   do   1621

  607   do   1632

  608 The noble soldier.   1634

ROWLEY, William.

  609 A new wonder, a woman never vext.   1632

  610 All's lost by lust.   1633

  611 A match at midnight.   1633

612 A shoemaker is a gentleman.   1638

613 The birth of Merlin.   1662

       The world tost at tennis.   See Middleton.

       A fair quarrel.   See Middleton.

       The Changeling.   See Middleton.

       The Spanish gipsey.   See Middleton.

       The old law.   See Middleton.

       The witch of Edmonton.   See Ford.

       Fortune by land and sea.   See Heywood.

       A cure for a cuckald.   See Webster.

       The Thracian wonder.   See Webster.

RUTTER, JOSEPH.

614 The shepherd's holiday.   1635

615 The Cid.   Part I.   1637

616   do   1650

617 The Cid.   Part II.   1640

SACKVILLE, THOMAS.

618 Gorboduc.   (Ferrex and Porrex.)   1565

619   do   1569

620   do   1571

621   do   1590

SADLER, Anthony.

622 The subjects' joy for the king's restoration. 1660

SAMPSON, William.

623 The vow breaker. 1636

Herod and Antipater. See Markham.

SAVILE, John.

624 King James his entertainment at Theobalds. 1603

SHAKESPEARE, William.

625 Works. 1623
626 do 1632
627 do 1663
628 do 1664
629 do 1685
630 Romeo and Juliet. 1597
631 do 1599
632 do 1609
633 do n. d.
634 do 1637
635 Richard II. 1597
636 do 1598
637 do 1608(2)

638	Richard II.		1615
639	do		1634
640	do		1681
641	Richard III.		1597
642	do		1598
643	do		1602
644	do		1605
645	do		1612
646	do		1622
647	do		1629
648	do		1634
649	do		1700
650	Henry IV. Part I.		1598
651	do		1599
652	do		1604
653	do		1608
654	do		1613
655	do		1622
656	do		1632
657	do		1639
658	Titus Andronicus.		1600
659	do		1611
660	do		1686
661	Merchant of Venice.	Roberts.	1600

662	Merchant of Venice.	Hayes.	1600
663	do		1637
664	do		1652
665	Love's labour's lost.		1598
666	do		1631
667	Henry V.		1600
668	do		1602
669	do		1608
670	Much ado about nothing.		1600
671	Henry IV. Part II.		1600
672	Midsummer night's dream.	Fisher.	1600
673	do	Roberts.	1600
674	Merry wives of Windsor.		1602
675	do		1619
676	do		1630
677	Hamlet.		1603
678	do		1604
679	do		1605
680	do		1611
681	do		n. d.
682	do		1637
683	do		1676
684	do		1685
685	do		1695

686	Hamlet.	1703
687	King Lear.	1608
688	do	1608
689	do	1655
690	Troilus and Cressida.	1609
691	do	1609
692	Pericles.	1609
693	do	1609
694	do	1611
695	do	1619
696	do	1630
697	do	1635
698	Othello.	1622
699	do	1630
700	do	1655
701	do	1687
702	do	1695
703	The taming of the shrew.	1631
704	Macbeth.	1674
705	do	1687
706	do	1695
707	do	1710
708	Julius Caesar.	1684
709	Henry the fourth, altered by Betterton.	1700

SHARPE, LEWIS.

  710 The noble stranger.   1640

SHARPHAM, EDWARD.

  711 The Fleire.   1607

  712   do   1610

  713   do   1615

  714   do   1621

  715 Cupid's whirligig.   1607

  716   do   1611

  717   do   1616

  718   do   1630

SHEPPARD, S.

  719 The committee man curried.   1647

SHIRLEY, HENRY.

  720 The martyred soldier.   1638

SHIRLEY, JAMES.

  721 The wedding.   1629

  722   do   1633

  723   do   1660

  724 The grateful servant.   1630

  725   do   1637

726	The grateful servant.	n. d.
727	The school of compliment.	1631
728	do	1633
729	do	1637
730	do	1667
731	The changes.	1632
732	Honor and Riches. ⎫	1633
733	Honoria and Mammon. ⎬	1659
734	The witty fair one.	1633
735	The bird in the cage.	1633
736	The triumph of peace.	1633
737	do	1633
738	do	1633
739	The traitor.	1635
740	do	1638
741	Hyde Park.	1637
742	The lady of pleasure.	1637
743	The young admiral.	1637
744	The example.	1637
745	The gamester.	1637
746	The Duke's mistress.	1638
747	The royal master.	1638
748	Chabot. (With Chapman.)	1639
749	The ball. (With Chapman.)	1639

750	The maid's revenge.	1639
751	The opportunity.	1640
752	Love's cruelty.	1640
753	The coronation.	1640
754	The humorous courtier.	1640
755	Arcadia.	1640
756	St. Patrick for Ireland.	1640
757	The constant maid. (Love will find out the way.)	1640
758	do	1661
759	do	1667
760	Cupid and death.	1653
761	do	1659
762	The gentleman of Venice.	1655
763	do	1655
764	The politician.	1655
765	do	1655

766 Six new plays: viz.: Brothers. Sisters. Doubtful heir. Imposture. Cardinal. Court Secret. } 1653

767 Two plays: viz.: The Constant Maid. St. Patrick for Ireland. } 1657

SMITH, WILLIAM *or* WENTWORTH.

768 The Hector of Germany.　　　　1615

SQUIRE, John.

769 The triumphs of peace.   1620

STEPHENS, *or* SWALLOW, John.

770 Cynthia's revenge.   1613

STILL, John.

771 Gammer Gurton's needle.   1575

772   do   1661

STRODE, William.

773 The floating island.   1655

SUCKLING, Sir John.

774 Aglaura.   1638

775 The discontented colonel.   (Brennoralt.)   n. d.

SWINHOE, Gilbert.

776 The unhappy fair Irene.   1658

TAILOR, Robert.

777 The hog hath lost his pearl.   1614

TATHAM, John.

778 Love crowns the end.   1640

779   do   1657

780	The distracted state.	1651
781	The Scots Figaries.	1652
782	London's triumphs.	1657
783	do	1658
784	do	1659
785	London's glory.	1660
786	The royal oak.	1660
787	The rump.	1660
788	London's triumphs.	1661
789	Neptune's address to Charles II.	1661
790	Aqua triumphalis.	1662
791	Londinium triumphans.	1663
792	London's triumphs.	1664
793	Knavery in all trades.	1664

TAYLOR, JOHN.

794	England's comfort, and London's joy.	1641
795	The triumphs of fame and honor.	1634

TOMKIS, THOMAS.

796	Albumazar.	1615
797	do	1634
798	do	1668

TOURNEUR, Cyril.

  799 The revenger's tragedy.   1607

  800   do   1608

  801 The atheist's tragedy.   1611

  802   do   1612

TOWNSEND, Aurelian.

  803 Albion's triumph.   1631

  804 Tempe restored.   1631

UDALL, Nicholas.

  805 Ralph Roister Doister.   (1566)

WAGER, Lewis.

  806 The repentance of Mary Magdalen.   1566

  807   do   1567

WAGER, W.

  808 The longer thou livest the more fool thou art.   (1570)

WAPULL, George.

  809 The tide tarrieth no man.   1576

WEBSTER, John.

  810 Sir Thomas Wyat. (With Dekker.)   1607

  811   do   1612

812	Westward Hoe. (With Dekker.)	1607
813	Northward Hoe. (With Dekker.)	1607
814	The white devil.	1612
815	do	1631
816	do	1665
817	do	1672
818	The Duchess of Malfi.	1623
819	do	1640
820	do	n. d.
821	The devil's law case.	1623
822	Monuments of honor.	1624
823	Appius and Virginia.	1654
824	do	1659
825	do	1679
826	A cure for a cuckold. (With Rowley.)	1661
827	The Thracian wonder. (With Rowley.)	1661

(Nos. 826 and 827 are sometimes bound together with a general
title-page added.)

The malcontent. See Marston.

WHETSTONE, GEORGE.

828	Promus and Cassandra.	1578

WILKINS, GEORGE.

829	The miseries of enforced marriage.	1697

830 The miseries of enforced marriage.   1611

831   do   1629

832   do   1637

WILLAN, LEONARD.

833 Astrea; or, true love's mirror.   1651

WILMOT, ROBERT.

834 Tancred and Gismond.   1591

835   do   1592

WILSON, J.

836 Andronicus Comnenus.   1664

WILSON, ROBERT.

837 The three ladies of London.   1584

838   do   1592

839 The three lords and three ladies of London.   1590

840 The pedlar's prophecy.   1595

841 The cobbler's prophecy.   1594

WOODES, NATHANIEL.

842 The conflict of conscience.   1581

YARRINGTON, ROBERT.

  843 Two lamentable tragedies.   1601

ZOUCH, RICHARD.

  844 The sophister.   1639

Anonymous and Wrongly Attributed Plays.

845 Certaine devises and shewes presented to her Maj-
  estie by the gentlemen of Grayes Inne, at her
  highnesse Court in Greenwich, the twenty-eighth
  day of Februarie, in the thirtieth yeare of her
  Majesties most happy raigne.   8vo. 1587

846 Gratiae Theatrales: or, a choice Ternary of English plays, composed upon especial occasions,
  by several ingenious persons.
      Contents: The London Maid. By T. W.
              The marriage broker. By M. W.
              Grim, the Collier of Croydon.   12mo. 1662

847 Actaeon and Diana.   n. d.

848   do   1656

849 Alphonsus, Emperor of Germany.   1654

850 Andromana; or the merchant's wife. By J. S. 1660

851 Andronicus: a tragedy.   1661

852 Appius and Virginia. By R. B.   1575

853 Arden of Feversham.   1592

854   do   1599

855   do   1633

856 Arraignment of Paris.   1584

857	Band, Cuff, and Ruff.	1615
858	do	1661
859	Exchange ware.	1615
860	Bloody banquet.	1639
861	Bottom the weaver, The merry conceited humors of.	1661
862	Caesar and Pompey, Tragedy of.	n. d.
863	do	1607
864	Captain Stukeley.	1605
865	Charles I. Famous tragedy of King Charles I. basely butchered.	1649
866	Contention between liberality and prodigality.	1602
867	Contention betwixt the two famous houses of York and Lancaster.	1594
868	do	1600
869	do	1600
870	do	n. d.
871	Costly whore.	1633
872	Cromwell's conspiracy.	1660
873	Cromwell, Lord.	1602
874	do	1613
875	Cruel war.	1643
876	Cruelty of the Spaniards in Peru.	1658
877	Damon and Pithias.	1571
878	do	1582

879	Darius.		1565
880	Drake, The history of Sir Francis.		1569
881	Edward III. (Attributed to Marlowe.)		1596
882	do		1599
883	do		1609
884	do		1612
885	do		1617
886	do		1625
887	Entertainment of King Charles, June 15, 1633.	Edinb.	1633
888	Entertainment to the Queen's Majesty at Elvetham.		1591
889	Every woman in her humor.		1609
890	Extravagant shepherd. A pastoral comedy. By T. R.		1654
891	Fair Em.		n. d.
892	do		1631
893	Fair maid of Bristol.		1605
894	Famous victories of Henry V.		1598
895	do		1617
896	Flowers, Masque of.		1614
897	Florimene, Pastoral of.		1635
898	Gesta Grayorum : or, the history of the high and mighty prince, Henry Prince of Purpoole, Arch-Duke of Stapulia and Bernardia, &c.		1688

899	Ghost; or the woman wears the breeches.	1653
900	Gossip's brawl; or the woman wears the breeches.	1655
901	Hectors: or, the false challenge.	1656
902	Histriomastix; or the player whipped.	1610
903	Honest lawyer. By S. S.	1616
904	How a man may choose a good wife from a bad.	1602
905	do	1605
906	do	1621
907	do	1630
908	do	1634
909	Impatient poverty. A new interlude.	1560
910	Jack Drum's entertainment.	1601
911	do	1616
912	do	1618
913	Jack Juggler.	(1563)
914	Jack Straw.	1593
915	do	1604
916	Jacob and Esau.	1568
917	John, The troublesome reign of King.	1591
918	do	1611
919	do	1622
920	King and Queen's entertainment at Richmond.	1636
921	Knack (A) to know a knave.	1594

922	Knack (A) to know an honest man.	1596
923	Knave (A) in grain new vampt. By T. D.	1640
924	Lady Alimony.	1659
925	Larum (A) for London.	1602
926	Leir, True chronicle history of King.	1605
927	Lingua.	1607
928	do	n. d.
929	do	1617
930	do	1622
931	do	1632
932	do	1657
933	Locrine.	1595
934	London prodigal. (Attributed to Shakespeare.)	1605
935	London's love to the royal Prince Henry.	1610
936	London chanticleers.	1659
937	Look about you.	1600
938	Luminalia ; or, the festival of light.	1637
939	Lust's dominion. (Attributed to Marlowe.)	1657
940	Lusty Juventus, An interlude called. W. Copland.	(c. 1560)
941	do Abraham Vele.	(c. 1560)
942	Maid's metamorphosis.	1600
943	Marcus Tullius Cicero.	1651
944	Merry devil of Edmonton.	1608
945	do	1612

946	Merry devil of Edmonton.	1617
947	do	1626
948	do	1631
949	do	1655
950	Mucedorus.	1598
951	do	1606
952	do	1610
953	do	1611
954	do	1613
955	do	1615
956	do	1618
957	do	1619
958	do	1626
959	do	1634
960	do	1639
961	do	1668
962	do	n. d.
963	Nero, Tragedy of.	1624
964	do	1633
965	Nero, Tragedy of Claudius Tiberius.	1607
966	New custom. (Interlude.)	1573
967	News out of the west.	1647
968	Nice wanton, A pretty interlude called.	1560
969	Nobody and somebody.	(1607)

970	Oldcastle, Sir John.		1600
971	do		1600
972	Orgula; or, the fatal error. By L. W.		1658
973	Pathomachia; or, the battle of affections.		1630
974	Petronius Maximus, The famous history of. By W. S.		1619
975	Prince of Prigs' revels. By J. S.		1651
976	Puritan, The.		1607
977	Queen, (The,) or, the excellency of her sex.		1653
978	Queen Hester. A new interlude.		1561
979	Rare triumph of love and fortune.		1589
980	Rebellion of Naples.		1649
981	do		1651
982	Revenge for honour. (Attributed to Chapman.)		1654
983	Return from Parnassus.		1606
984	Richard Duke of York, True tragedy of.		1595
985	do		1600
986	Richard the third.		1594
987	Robin Hood.	W. Copland.	n. d.
988	do	E. White.	n. d.
989	Royal passage of her Majesty to Whitehall.		1604
990	Selimus, Emperor of the Turks, Tragical reign of.		1594
991	do		1638
992	Sir Cliomon.		1599
993	Sir Giles Goosecap.		1606

994	Sir Giles Goosecap.	1636
995	do	n. d.
996	Soliman and Perseda. (Attributed to Kyd.)	1599
997	do	n. d.
998	Spanish bawd.	1631
999	Swetnam the woman-hater.	1620
1000	Taming of a shrew.	1594
1001	do	1596
1002	do	1607
1003	Titus, or, the palm of Christian courage.	1644
1004	Tom Tyler and his wife.	1661
1005	Trial of chivalry: with the life and death of Cavaliero Dick Bowyer.	1605
1006	do	1605
1007	Trial of treasure. (Interlude.)	1567
1008	Two merry milk maids. By J. C.	1620
1009	do	1661
1010	Two wise men and all the rest fools.	1619
1011	Unfortunate usurper.	1663
1012	Ungrateful favorite.	1664
1013	Valiant Scot. By J. W.	1637
1014	Valiant Welshman. By R. A.	1615
1015	do	1663
1016	Warning for fair women.	1599

1017	Wars of Cyrus.		1594
1018	Warwick (Guy), Earl of.		1661
1019	Weakest (The) goeth to the wall.		1600
1020	do		1618
1021	Wily beguiled.		1606
1022	do		1623
1023	do		1630
1024	do		1635
1025	do		1638
1026	Wine, beer, and ale.		1629
1027	do		1630
1028	do		1658
1029	Wisdom of Dr. Dodipoll.		1600
1030	Wit of a woman.		1604
1031	Woman is a weather-cock.		1612
1032	Work for cutlers.		1615
1033	Yorkshire tragedy.		1608
1034	do		1619
1035	Youth, The interlude of.	John Waley.	n. d.
1036	do	W. Copland.	n. d.

Translated Plays.

BERNARD, RICHARD.

1037	The comedies of Terence.	1588
1038	do	1607
1039	do	1621
1040	do	1641

CHEEKE, HENRY.

1041	Free will. (From the Italian.)	(c. 1560)

DANCER, JOHN.

1042	Aminta. A pastoral. (From Tasso.)	1660

DYMOCK, CHARLES.

1043	Il pastor fido. (From Guarini.)	1602
1044	do	1633

FANSHAWE, SIR R.

1045	Il Pastor Fido. (From Guarini.)	1647
1046	do	1648
1047	do	1664

1048 Il Pastor Fido.   (From Guarini.)   1676

1049 Querer por solo querer: to love only for love's sake.

    (From Mendoza.)   1670

1050   do   1671

GOLDSMITH, Francis.

1051 Hugo Grotius his Sophompaneas.   1652

HEYWOOD, Jasper.

1052 Troas.   (From Seneca.)   n. d.

1053   do   n. d.

1054 Thyestes.   (From Seneca.)   1560

1055 Hercules Furens.   (From Seneca.)   1561

HOOLE, Charles.

1056 The six comedies of Terence in English and Latin.   1663

KYFFIN, Maurice.

1057 Andria.   (From Terence.)   1588

NEWMAN, Thomas.

1058 The Eunuch.   (From Terence.)   1627

1059 Andria.   (From Terence.)   1628

NUCE, Thomas.

1060 Octavia.   (From Seneca.)   (1566)

NEVILE, ALEXANDER.

   1061 Oedipus. (From Seneca.)   1563

PEMBROKE, COUNTESS OF.

   1062 Antonius. (From the French.)   1592
   1063   do   1595

PRESTWICH, EDMUND.

   1064 Hippolytus. (From Seneca.)   1651

RANDOLPH, THOMAS.

   1065 Hey for honesty, down with knavery. (From
          Aristophanes.)   1651

REYNOLDS, JOHN.

   1066 Aminta. A pastoral. (From Tasso.)   1628

SANDYS, GEORGE.

   1067 Christ's passion. (From Grotius.)   1640
   1068   do   1687

SHERBURNE, SIR EDWARD.

   1069 Medea.   (From Seneca.)   1648
   1070 Troades, or the royal captives. (From Seneca.)   1679

STUDLEY, John.

   1071 Agamemnon.   (From Seneca.)   1566

         Medea.   (From Seneca.)   1566

WASE, Christopher.

   1072 Electra of Sophocles.   1649

Anonymous Translators.

www.ingramcontent.com/pod-product-compliance
Lightning Source LLC
Chambersburg PA
CBHW021515090426
42739CB00007B/624